W9-CBB-301

SURVIVORS FROM EARTH'S DISTANT PAST

REBECCA E. HIRSCH

M MILLBROOK PRESS / MINNEAPOLIS

To everyone, everywhere in the world, taking action to save animals

Millbrook Press™
An imprint of Lerner Publishing Group, Inc.
241 First Avenue North
Minneapolis, MN 55401 USA

For reading levels and more information, look up this title at www.lernerbooks.com.

Designed by Danielle Carnito.
Main body text set in Jonhston ITC Std.
Typeface provided by International Typeface Corp.

Library of Congress Cataloging-in-Publication Data

Names: Hirsch, Rebecca E., author.
Title: Living fossils : survivors from Earth's distant past / Rebecca E. Hirsch.
Description: Minneapolis : Millbrook Press, [2020] | Includes bibliographical references and index. | Audience: Ages 8–14. | Audience: Grades 4–6. | Summary: "Blue-blooded crabs? Platypus that sting? One-hundred-year-old reptiles? Meet some of nature's longest-surviving species! Discover the stories of these incredible animals and find out how they help scientists piece together evolutionary history"— Provided by publisher.
Identifiers: LCCN 2019049426 (print) | LCCN 2019049427 (ebook) | ISBN 9781541581272 (library binding) | ISBN 9781728401508 (ebook)
Subjects: LCSH: Living fossils—Juvenile literature. | Animals, Fossil—Juvenile literature. | Evolution—Juvenile fiction.
Classification: LCC QL88.5 .H57 2020 (print) | LCC QL88.5 (ebook) | DDC 591.3/8—dc23

LC record available at https://lccn.loc.gov/2019049426
LC ebook record available at https://lccn.loc.gov/2019049427

Manufactured in the United States of America
1-47326-47953-4/16/2020

CONTENTS

SLIME SHOOTERS

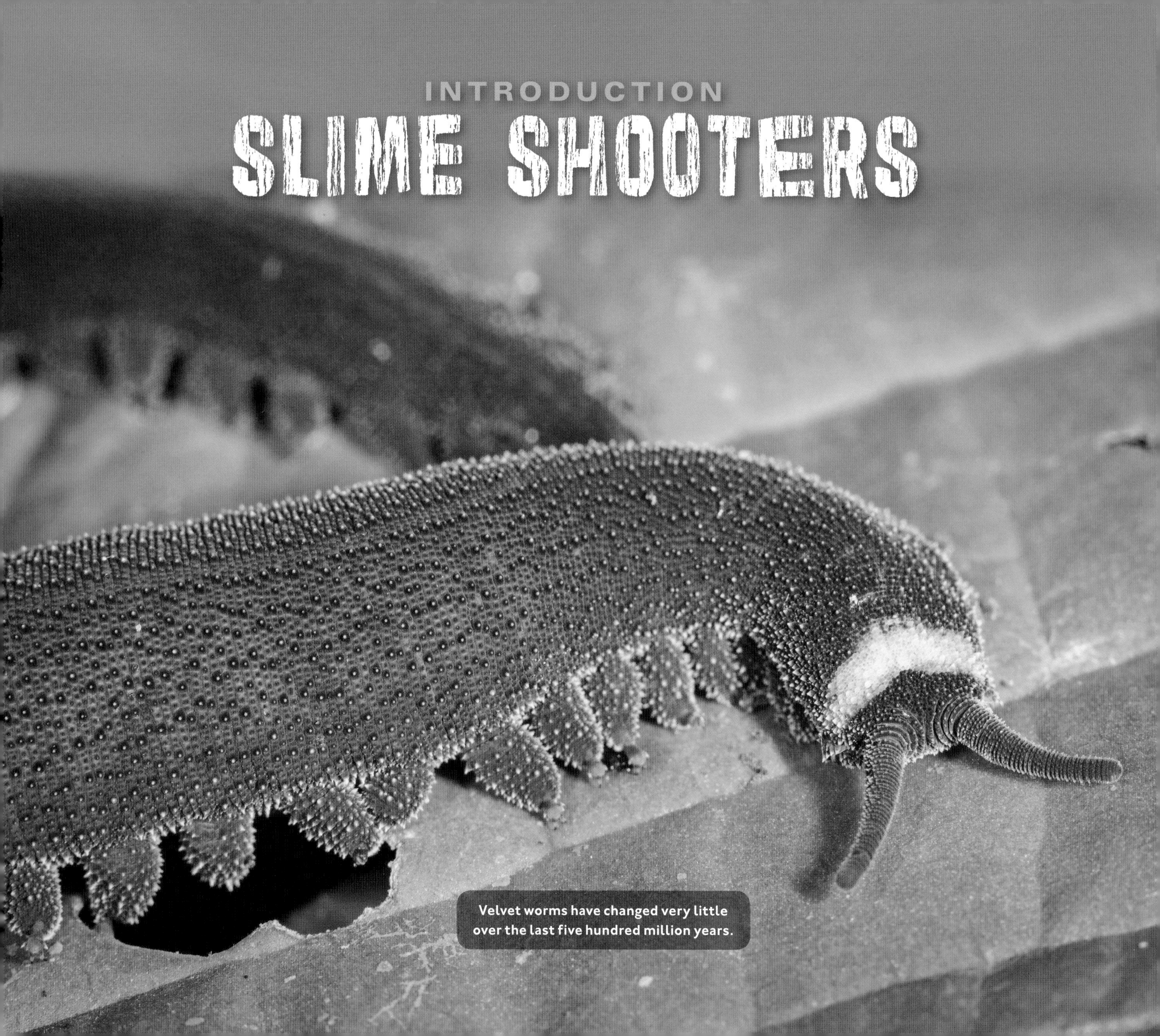

Velvet worms have changed very little over the last five hundred million years.

Something strange is roaming the New Zealand rain forest. You've heard about this odd creature. You are here in the forest to see it for yourself. You step carefully along the path.

The only sound is the chirping of birds high in the trees and the tramp of your boots on the soft earth. Your fingers tighten on your hatchet.

The creatures, you've been told, have no bones. Their bodies are fluid-filled sacs. Their stubby legs look like blobs. They have no eyes, but they can sense movement.

And they are hungry. When they detect prey, nozzles pop out of their heads. Sticky slime shoots out and immobilizes their target. After their prey is ensnared, they bite into it, injecting saliva to liquefy its insides. Then they eat.

A rotting log lies beside the path. You stop walking. With both hands, you lift the hatchet and sink the blade into the soft wood. You chip away at the log until you see the creatures. Velvet worms. They are the size of large caterpillars but oddly liquid in their movements. Fortunately, they pose no threat to you. Their slime is for capturing smaller prey, like beetles.

Meet one of the world's most amazing animals. You'll find velvet worms in damp forests around the equator and in the Southern Hemisphere, creeping through leaf litter or crawling inside rotten logs. These slime shooters have been prowling the planet for five hundred million years.

On Earth most species appear, live for a time, and then die out. Out of all the species that have ever lived on our planet, more than 99 percent are now extinct.

But a few species have stuck around. They have remained on Earth almost unchanged for millions and millions of years—since the time of the dinosaurs. Some have roamed since the dawn of animal life. The continents have shifted. Oceans have risen and fallen. Meteorites have slammed into the planet. Creatures near and far have gone extinct. But these survivors have kept going.

How did they do it? Can they tell us what life was like in the prehistoric past? And will they survive into the future?

Lace up your hiking boots, and get ready for a strange journey. The world's oldest creatures are weirder than you think.

CHAPTER 1

THE STORY OF LIFE

The first living things on Earth were single cells that lived in the ocean, just as these phytoplankton do.

Life on Earth began 3.5 billion years ago. In the beginning, every living thing was tiny, made of only a single cell. All life resided in the sea. For nearly 3 billion years, that's the way life stayed—tiny, single-celled, and floating in the ocean.

Then, between 730 and 630 million years ago, early animals appeared. Small jellyfishlike creatures swam in the sea. Tiny, wormlike animals squirmed on the ocean floor.

Between 570 and 530 million years ago, many new and strange animals appeared in the sea. Scientists call this the Cambrian explosion, a burst of new life. Many of these animals had hard shells and new body plans, with heads, tails, and limbs. There was the armored trilobite (TRYE-luh-byte) with a flattened, segmented body. There was the five-eyed *Opabinia* (o-pa-BIN-ee-ah), with a nose like a fire hose and a flexible armed claw attached to its head. There was *Aysheaia* (eye-SHAY-ah), as big as a caterpillar, but with a fluid-filled-sac for a body and many stubby legs that looked like blobs.

SURVIVAL OF THE FITTEST

Where did these animals come from? They evolved, or changed over time, from earlier life-forms.

We have British naturalist Charles Darwin to thank for helping the world understand how evolution works. In 1859 he published his far-reaching ideas about how living things evolve in his book *On the Origin of Species*.

Darwin proposed that every living thing on Earth is related to every other living thing—including human beings. We are all connected in a great chain of life, all the way back to the first single-celled organism.

Darwin explained that new livings things arise by a natural process, and this process starts with heredity. All living things evolve by passing on traits to their offspring. Some traits improve an animal's chances of survival. For

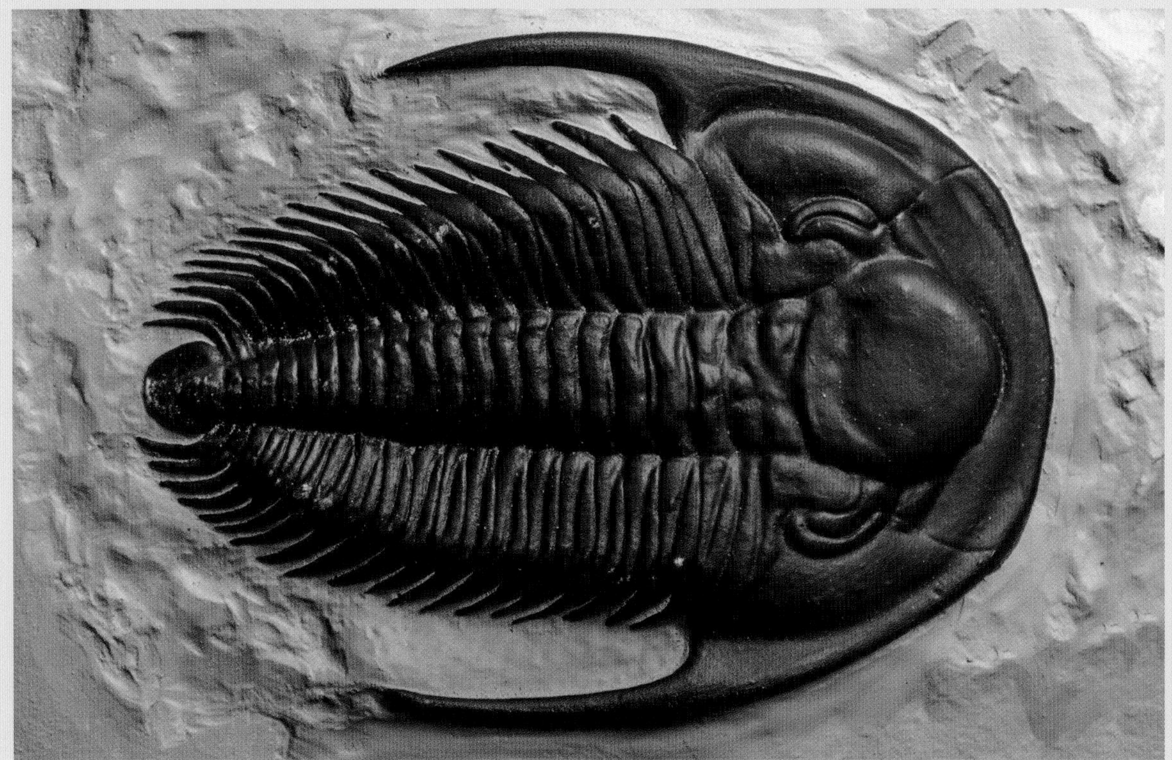

Most animals that arose during the Cambrian explosion, like this fossilized trilobite, have long since disappeared from Earth.

example, a hard outer body could protect a sea creature from being eaten. If that animal passes on this helpful trait to its young, then its children are more likely to survive and become parents themselves. As the generations pass, animals that have inherited this helpful trait may flourish. Animals that lack this helpful trait might reproduce less and even die out. Darwin called this process natural selection, or survival of the fittest.

Generation by generation, changes in traits can build up. Over a long time, these changes can produce entirely new kinds of living things—such as trilobites, *Opabinia*, and *Aysheaia*.

What happened to the animals of the Cambrian explosion? Many disappeared without a trace. *Opabinia* went extinct without leaving any descendants. So you won't see any five-eyed creatures with a claw on their head wandering around today. Others went extinct, but their relatives survived and changed. The trilobites are long gone, but their relatives live among us in many forms—insects and spiders, centipedes and millipedes, and crabs and crayfish.

But a few strange creatures from the Cambrian explosion survived, and they are still around in nearly identical form. *Aysheaia* looks almost exactly like the velvet worms that patrol tropical forests today.

Darwin puzzled over animals like this, ones that look so similar to their ancient relatives. He called them living fossils, organisms that bear a striking resemblance to their long-extinct relatives that swam, scuttled, or crawled across the prehistoric Earth.

But *living fossil* is not an actual scientific term, even though many scientists use it. For them, calling something a living fossil expresses their surprise and wonder over how a creature can look so much like its ancient relatives.

However, some scientists don't like that name. They say that calling something a living fossil implies the species is stuck in the past, as if it had stopped evolving, as if it has been marching in place. And that's not the way evolution works, these scientists point out. *All* life changes over time. So while a living animal might look similar to its ancient relatives, it could have subtle changes or new features. For example, while *Aysheaia* looked nearly the same as velvet worms, it lacked the slime-shooting nozzles.

Whatever you call these animals, why should we pay attention to them? What's so important about so-called living fossils?

These odd animals have much to teach us. They can give us clues about what traits can help a species survive for a long time. They can bring us breakthroughs in medicine and the treatment of diseases. They can help us solve some of the deepest mysteries about life—how

RECORD IN THE ROCKS

Fossils are the remains of past life. They may be bones or shells or tracks in the mud. Fossils usually show up in sedimentary rocks, the most common rocks on Earth's surface. These rocks are formed from layers of sand and mud that build up, get compacted, and cement into rock over time. The layers form in order, younger layers building on top of older layers.

Fossils in layers of rock show how life has changed over time. The oldest rocks, the bottom layers, contain traces of single cells. Moving up the layers, early animals appear. You'll see snails and trilobites and even occasionally the soft bodies of wormlike creatures. Moving higher, you'll find fossils that look similar to many animals alive today—fish, then amphibians, and then reptiles. Then you'll find fossils of dinosaurs. Near the top, you'll see birds and mammals.

But the fossil record has entire pages missing. Most animals don't form a fossil when they die. Usually a scavenger eats them, or their body decays without leaving a trace. And soft-bodied creatures are less likely to leave a fossil. This creates gaps in the fossil record.

Survivors can fill in some of the story. Animals that are the living descendants of ancient lineages can fill in clues to the past. By studying them closely, we can begin to learn the secrets of life on Earth and how it has changed over time.

it was in the past, how it is now, and how it came to be that way.

LIFE ON LAND

After the Cambrian explosion, life continued to evolve. By 525 million years ago, fish with eel-like bodies were swimming in the ocean. Next came sharks and many other new kinds of fish.

After that came a pivotal moment in the history of life: animals crawled out of the water and onto land. The first land animals were invertebrates (soft-bodied animals with no bones), such as insects and spiders. By four hundred million years ago, vertebrates (animals with backbones) had joined them, when fish evolved into four-footed creatures that could walk.

These four-footed land animals continued to change. Over millions of years, they became amphibians, such as frogs and salamanders. They became reptiles, such as turtles, crocodiles, snakes, and lizards. One reptile group evolved into dinosaurs. Dinosaurs would rule on land for millions and millions of years.

Another reptile group evolved into mammals, animals with fur that fed their babies milk. Early mammals were small, no bigger than a squirrel. With dinosaurs stomping around in daylight, they came out at night to avoid becoming a dinosaur's lunch.

That's the way the world stood sixty-five million years ago, when something that looked like a star appeared in the sky. Over a few days, the object grew brighter. Only it wasn't a star. It was a meteorite 6 miles (10 km) wide, and

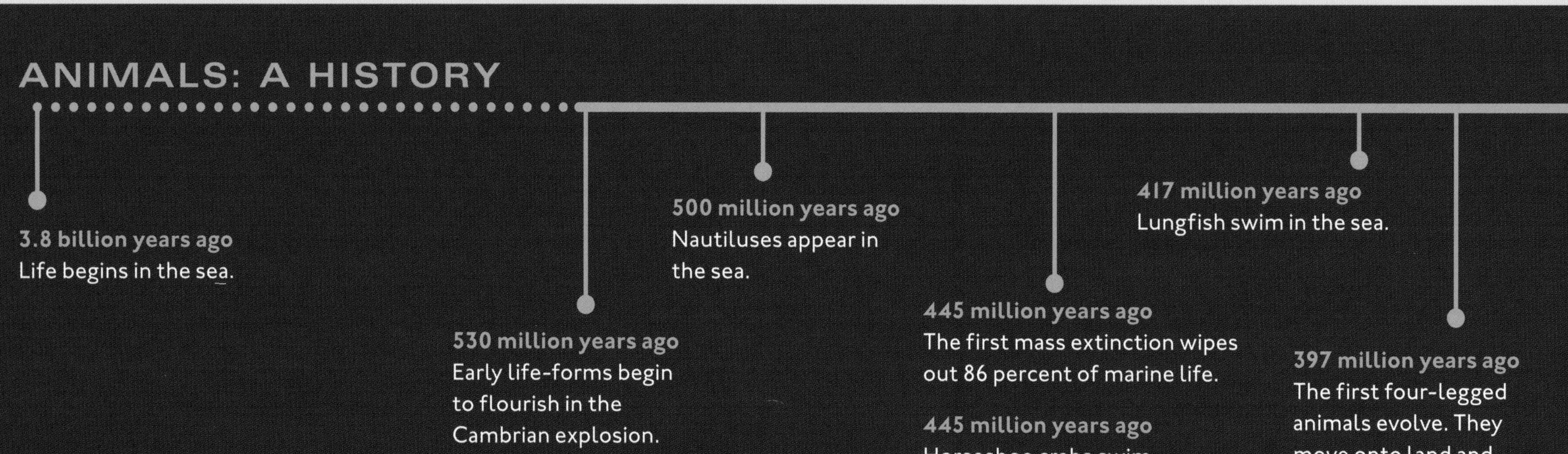
ANIMALS: A HISTORY
3.8 billion years ago
Life begins in the sea.
530 million years ago
Early life-forms begin to flourish in the Cambrian explosion.
500 million years ago
Nautiluses appear in the sea.
445 million years ago
The first mass extinction wipes out 86 percent of marine life.
445 million years ago
Horseshoe crabs swim in the ocean.
417 million years ago
Lungfish swim in the sea.
397 million years ago
The first four-legged animals evolve. They move onto land and become amphibians, reptiles, and mammals.

it was speeding toward Earth at 45,000 miles (72,400 km) per hour.

The meteorite crashed into a shallow sea near the Yucatán Peninsula of Mexico. The impact sent giant tidal waves churning up the coastline. It threw trillions of tons of dust into the air. The debris that rose up was glowing hot, some of it hotter than the surface of the sun. As winds blew the smoldering dust around the globe, most of the world's forests went up in flames, and smoke choked the skies. With so much dust, debris, and soot in the air, the planet grew dark for months.

Most of the world's land plants died at that time, unable to carry out photosynthesis. Phytoplankton, tiny plants that live in the ocean, died too. Without plants, Earth's food chains collapsed. About 75 percent of all species went extinct. Some mammals made it through. Most of the dinosaurs died, and their reign came to a close. Only one group of dinosaurs survived and still lives among us. We know them as birds.

An event like this is called a mass extinction. During a mass extinction, large numbers of species die out in a short period of time. There have been five mass extinctions in Earth's history. The meteorite that killed the dinosaurs was the most recent one. While that event may have been bad for the dinosaurs, it allowed mammals to evolve, diversify, and flourish—including human beings.

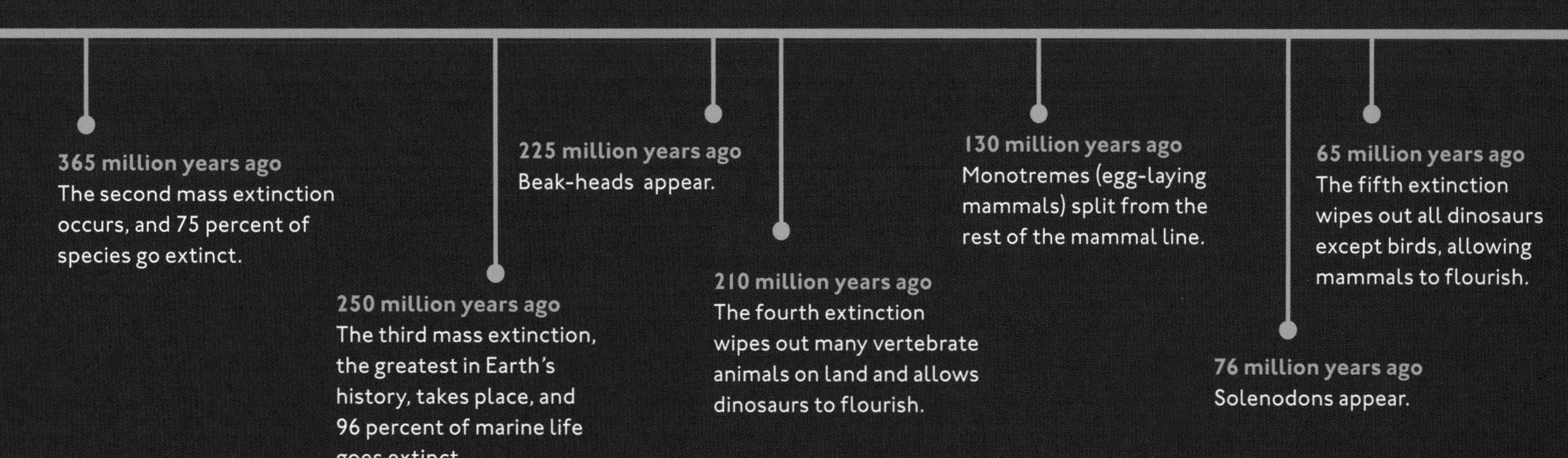
365 million years ago
The second mass extinction occurs, and 75 percent of species go extinct.
250 million years ago
The third mass extinction, the greatest in Earth's history, takes place, and 96 percent of marine life goes extinct.
225 million years ago
Beak-heads appear.
210 million years ago
The fourth extinction wipes out many vertebrate animals on land and allows dinosaurs to flourish.
130 million years ago
Monotremes (egg-laying mammals) split from the rest of the mammal line.
76 million years ago
Solenodons appear.
65 million years ago
The fifth extinction wipes out all dinosaurs except birds, allowing mammals to flourish.

CHAPTER 2

GREEN EGGS AND SAND

With its armored body and spiky tail, a horseshoe crab looks like a creature from an alien world.

It is a warm evening in late spring. As the full moon rises, waves crash along a beach in the Delaware Bay. Each wave leaves behind a rim of bubbles and a bit of seaweed on damp sand. The tide is coming in.

Something else is coming in too.

Out of the surf rise hundreds of dark, armored creatures. They glide onto the sand like the tanks of an invading army. The big ones look like hubcaps with pointy swords for tails. The small ones hang onto the big ones. Up the beach they creep, moonlight glistening on their shells.

NAME: horseshoe crab

SCIENTIFIC NAME: Limulidae (lim-YUH-luh-day) family

SIZE: up to 19 inches (48 cm) long

WHERE CAN YOU FIND IT? Atlantic coastline of North America, coastlines of South and Southeast Asia

HABITAT: shallow waters along the coast, beaches for spawning

SURVIVAL TACTIC: A horseshoe crab has ten eyes: seven eyes on its shell, another eye on its tail, and two eyes near its mouth. Two of these eyes become a *million* times more sensitive to light at night. That makes it possible for horseshoe crabs to see just as well at night as they can during the day.

The horseshoe crabs have arrived.

Horseshoe crabs have been spawning on beaches for the past 445 million years. They are among the planet's most ancient survivors.

For most of the year, horseshoe crabs live in shallow waters along the shore, eating worms and clams. But in springtime when the tide is at its highest, they crawl onto beaches from Maine to Florida and along parts of Mexico. Three other horseshoe crab species come ashore in Asia.

The big ones are females. Each female scoops out a nest in the damp sand near bits of seaweed at the high tide line. She lays about four thousand sticky green eggs in a cluster. During a single night, she lays up to five clusters of eggs. The smaller horseshoe crabs, the males, release sperm to fertilize the eggs.

As the tide goes out, the horseshoe crabs return to the sea. For the next few nights, they come back to the beach

In Cape May, New Jersey, horseshoe crabs come ashore to spawn each spring.

After spawning takes place, the sand is full of horseshoe crab eggs. These eggs are an important part of the food chain.

until each female has laid about eighty thousand eggs. All together, the horseshoe crabs on a single beach can leave behind *billions* of eggs.

Horseshoe crab eggs are an important part of the food chain. Migrating shorebirds show up at spawning time. The birds time their migration so they can gorge on horseshoe crab eggs. Some birds have come all the way from South America and must continue to their nesting grounds in the Arctic. They jab their sharp beaks into the damp sand, scrambling to fuel up on sticky green eggs. Some birds nearly double their weight before they flap away to finish their journey.

After about a month, the surviving eggs still left in the sand hatch. Tiny horseshoe crabs crawl out of the sand and head for the sea.

HARD TIMES FOR HORSESHOES

Horseshoe crabs are not true crabs. They are more closely related to spiders and scorpions. They even look spidery—if spiders had armor and tails and six pairs of legs each ending with a pincer. The tails look sharp but are not dangerous. Horseshoe crabs use them to steer underwater and flip themselves if they land on their backs in the sand.

These ancient creatures look weird on the outside, and they're just as weird inside. The blood that flows through their bodies has powerful, medicinal properties. These properties stem from the blood's unusual reaction to foreign bacteria. Thanks to these properties, horseshoe crab blood has kept countless people alive—maybe even you. The blood is so valuable that a quart is worth about $15,000.

But horseshoe crabs are in trouble. In the last few decades, fewer and fewer horseshoe crabs have been coming ashore. That worries scientists. Fewer horseshoe crabs means fewer eggs for migratory birds. That puts birds at risk. Birds that don't eat enough may not reach their nesting grounds. Fewer horseshoe crabs put people at risk too, since we depend on the lifesaving blood.

What is happening to the horseshoe crabs?

BLUE BLOODS

Horseshoe crab blood is blue and cloudy, like sports drink mixed with milk. The color comes from having copper in their blood, rather than iron, which is what you have. Copper turns blue when exposed to the air.

Their blood is extremely valuable due to a strange property. The blood has a powerful defense against foreign bacteria. Bacteria are tiny, single-celled organisms that live everywhere on Earth. If the wrong bacteria get inside a horseshoe crab through a wound, they could kill the animal. But horseshoe crab blood turns to stringy goo the instant it touches bacteria. This clot seals the wound, stops bacteria from entering, and keeps the horseshoe crab safe.

The clot is what makes horseshoe crab blood so valuable to people. It is why people catch horseshoe

Above: Jeak Ling Ding (*left*) and Bow Ho of the National University of Singapore studied a chemical that causes horseshoe crab blood to clot. *Right:* Horseshoe crabs are bled at the Charles River Laboratories in Charleston, South Carolina.

crabs, drive them to a blood bank, and draw some of their blood before returning the animals to the sea. They do this because bacteria are dangerous to people too. If bacteria get into our blood, the infection can cause fever and even death.

So how does horseshoe crab blood protect people from harmful bacteria? Medical companies use horseshoe crab blood to check the cleanliness of anything that might come in contact with our blood. They test needles before they are used on patients. They test devices like pacemakers before they are implanted in patients. If the test stays liquid, the devices are safe to be used in people. Astronauts even test spaceships for contamination before launching into space.

But harvesting blood may be harming horseshoe crab populations. In the US, roughly five hundred thousand horseshoe crabs are bled each year. Between 10 and 30 percent of those animals die during the process. More may die after the crabs are returned to the ocean. Harvesting horseshoe crab blood may be putting the population at risk.

That's not the only problem. Horseshoe crab blood is also very expensive. Some hospitals can't afford to use it. Which is why, in the 1980s, Jeak Ling Ding of the National

University of Singapore found herself squelching through swamps in search of horseshoe crabs.

Ding's husband and research partner, Bow Ho, had gotten a call from a hospital in Singapore. The hospital was having a problem with bacterial contamination, but horseshoe crab blood was too expensive. So Ding and Ho joined forces to see if they could make a cheaper substitute for the hospitals to use.

A substitute would not only help hospitals and their patients. It would also help horseshoe crabs. If Ding and Ho succeeded, horseshoe crabs would no longer be needed for medical testing.

So Ding and Ho headed to swamps on the northern coast of Singapore. Ding did not enjoy the swamps. "The mud is horrendous," she said, "It contains billions of disease-causing bacteria. One could easily fall into the mud. It's really gloopy."

They pulled Asian horseshoe crabs out of the muck and brought them to Ding's lab. They drained some of their blood, then released the crabs back into the swamp.

Now that they had some horseshoe crab blood, they needed to learn what substance in the blood detects bacteria. They discovered that a chemical, called factor C, was responsible. Next, they set out to make factor C in the laboratory.

The work was challenging. Bacteria lurk everywhere, even in a laboratory. If the blood in their tubes touched bacteria, it would turn to stringy slime and clot. They had to bake all the glassware at 437°F (225°C) for four hours. Only then would all traces of bacteria be destroyed.

Once Ding's student accidentally put blood into the wrong tube. Instant squishy goo! Ding found the student playing with the failed experiment. "He was bouncing it like a rubber ball up and down the corridor," she said.

After many mistakes, the team finally learned how to make synthetic factor C. No horseshoe crabs needed! But could their factor C detect bacteria? They had to put the substitute to the test. They found that their version worked even better than horseshoe crab blood.

After fifteen years of work, they had a substitute for blue blood. Their factor C went up for sale in 2000. "Then came the waiting and waiting," Ding said. Medical companies were reluctant to make the switch. What if the new product failed? That could put people's lives at risk. Ding turned to conservationists in the US, people who wanted to save horseshoe crabs and the shorebirds that need them. It took time, but the conservationists convinced the companies. In 2018 medical companies began using Ding's product.

This means that the harvest of horseshoe crab blood may be coming to a close. Ding is happy to see her lifesaving substitute being used to help people after all these years. She hopes that horseshoe crabs will keep crawling onto beaches each spring, as they have for millions of years. She hopes the birds will show up, too, and continue to feast on green eggs, far into the future.

CHAPTER 3

TANGLE OF TENTACLES

NAME: chambered nautilus

SCIENTIFIC NAME: *Nautilus pompilius* (NAWT-i-luhs pom-PIL-ee-uhs)

SIZE: up to 9 inches (23 cm) across

WHERE CAN YOU FIND IT? Indian and Pacific Oceans

HABITAT: coral reefs

SURVIVAL TACTIC: The spiraled shell of a nautilus is divided into chambers. The animal lives in the outermost chamber. The inner chambers are filled with gas to help a nautilus float in the water. A nautilus pumps liquid into the chambers when it wants to dive.

In the South Pacific Ocean, in the dark water at the bottom of a coral reef, something is stirring.

Over the mud and sand and rubble from the reef, a chambered nautilus creeps. It trails ninety rubbery tentacles from its tiger-striped shell. It sputters along by jet propulsion, spitting water out of a funnel beneath its mouth.

The slow-moving creature reaches the cliff-like wall of the reef. Up the reef it rises. Up, up, up. When it reaches the top of the reef, the sun has set. The water is nearly dark.

In the fading light, a titan triggerfish spies the nautilus. The fish circles, sizing up its prey. To the triggerfish, the nautilus looks like a tasty morsel. The nautilus senses danger. It pulls itself inside its shell and closes its leathery hood.

The triggerfish lunges and bites, but the nautilus floats free. The fish attacks again. But it cannot get a grip on the smooth, slippery shell. The triggerfish gives up and swims away.

Unharmed, the nautilus opens its hood. It is hungry. It slowly searches the reef, feeling and sniffing its way with a tangle of tentacles. The nautilus finds a shrimp and wraps its sticky tentacles around its prey. It pulls the shrimp into its mouth, and crunches down with its sharp jaws.

As dawn nears, the nautilus descends to deep water. Sunlight means danger from shell-breaking triggerfish, turtles, octopuses, and sharks. Deep, dark water means safety. The nautilus will hide at the bottom of the reef until night falls again.

PREHISTORIC PREDATORS

A chambered nautilus is a mollusk, related to clams and snails. Along with cuttlefish, squids, and octopuses, nautiluses are cephalopods. *Cephalopod* means "head-foot" because the feet (tentacles) are attached to the head. Nautiluses are the only living cephalopod with an external shell for protection.

Nautiluses have been bobbing in the ocean for five hundred million years. The first nautiluses had straight, pointy shells, like long party hats. Later, they developed spiral, tiger-striped shells. The shells protected them but also slowed them down.

For hundreds of millions of years, nautiluses prowled the prehistoric sea. There were thousands of nautilus species. They may have been slow, but they could chase down the many even slower ocean creatures. Nautiluses were top predators, the terrors of the seas.

As time passed, faster ocean predators evolved. There were sharks and fish, squids and octopuses. Slow-moving nautiluses became easy prey for these newer, faster killers. Through the ages, the number of nautilus species dwindled. Today, just six species survive. With so many predators swimming around, they hide in deep water by day. At night, they bob to the surface to hunt under cover of darkness.

A nautilus has up to ninety tentacles, which it uses to smell and to handle food.

ANCIENT ANIMAL, NEW TRICKS

After surviving on Earth for nearly five hundred million years, nautiluses may be facing their greatest challenge—humans. In the 1970s, people began fishing for the ancient animals. Fishermen lowered baited traps on ropes into coral reefs, hauled up nautiluses, and sold their shells to jewelers and shell shops. Millions of nautiluses died, their shells turned into souvenirs and trinkets.

"There are populations of nautiluses that are just gone now," says Jennifer Basil, a biologist at Brooklyn College. "They've been fished away."

Basil studies nautilus intelligence, and she keeps a dozen nautiluses in tanks in her laboratory. She believes we need to learn about these ancient cephalopods so we can better understand how to protect them.

Cephalopods are the brainiest of all invertebrates. Squids cooperate to hunt fish and communicate by changing the color and texture of their skin. Octopuses navigate mazes, use tools, and solve complex problems. Octopuses kept in laboratories are famous for their shenanigans. One laboratory octopus kept in a tank was known to short-circuit a nearby light by shooting water at it if the light was left on at night.

But what about nautiluses? Scientists have long believed these ancient shelled creatures are not nearly as smart as other cephalopods. Scientists thought that cephalopod intelligence had evolved more recently—long after nautiluses began jetting around.

But Basil suspected scientists were underestimating the nautilus. Together with her colleague Robyn Crook, she began putting nautilus smarts to the test.

Basil and Crook wanted to test the nautiluses' navigation abilities. In the ocean, nautiluses are very good at navigating the coral reef. "They remember good hiding spots," Basil said. "They're very good at hiding their eggs." Nautiluses hide their eggs to protect them from hungry predators. Their hiding spots are so ingenious that people rarely find nautilus eggs.

So the two women gave the animal species a navigation problem to solve. How would nautiluses do in a maze?

The maze was a circular, water-filled tank. A horizontal barrier separated the bright surface water from the dark, deeper water. The barrier had a nautilus-sized hole in it. Nautiluses don't like the light. The goal was to see if the creatures could find the hole and escape the light into deeper waters.

First came the training. Each nautilus was lowered into the well-lit part of the maze and given ten minutes to find the hole. Some found it on their own. Some were still bobbing around in brightly lit surface waters after ten minutes. By hand, researchers gently guided these lost animals into the hole.

It took only three trials for nautiluses to learn how the maze worked. Once they acquired this knowledge, all of the creatures jetted straight for the hole.

The nautiluses could even remember how the maze worked weeks later. When they hadn't been in the maze for two to three weeks, they still went straight for the hole. Basil said their maze learning and memory abilities rivaled those of octopuses.

The results reveal that nautiluses may be ancient, but they aren't dumb. Basil believes intelligence traces back to the early history of cephalopods. Perhaps nautiluses evolved big brains early in their history to survive in an ocean full of predators.

Basil says nautiluses are fascinating animals to study. Each nautilus in her lab has a unique personality. "It's like having a dozen teenagers with no common sense," says Basil. "They're always fighting over food and trying to go out the outlet pipe."

She believes these ancient animals have much to teach us—about how a creature very different from us thinks, about how intelligence evolves. "Even the strangest of animals can teach us something," she said. "It's important to protect them so they can continue to be themselves and we can continue to learn from them."

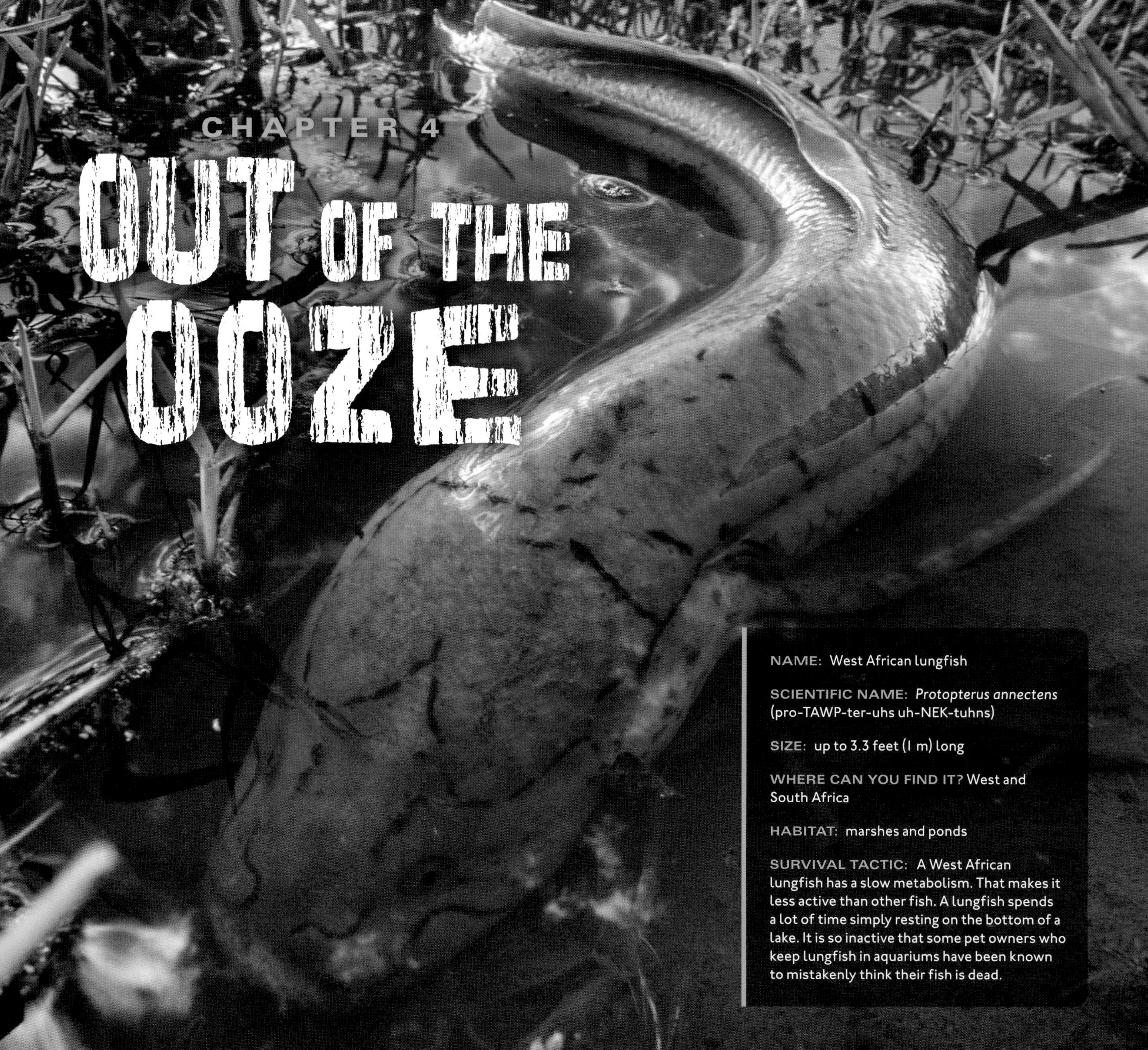

CHAPTER 4

OUT OF THE OOZE

NAME: West African lungfish

SCIENTIFIC NAME: *Protopterus annectens* (pro-TAWP-ter-uhs uh-NEK-tuhns)

SIZE: up to 3.3 feet (1 m) long

WHERE CAN YOU FIND IT? West and South Africa

HABITAT: marshes and ponds

SURVIVAL TACTIC: A West African lungfish has a slow metabolism. That makes it less active than other fish. A lungfish spends a lot of time simply resting on the bottom of a lake. It is so inactive that some pet owners who keep lungfish in aquariums have been known to mistakenly think their fish is dead.

On the edge of a marsh in West Africa, a fish flops in the muck. Its body is as long as a baseball bat. Its long, thin fins dangle like shoelaces in the mud.

No rain has fallen for months. The marsh has slowly dried into a puddle. For an ordinary fish, this would be a life-threatening situation.

But this is no ordinary fish. It is a West African lungfish, and it can breathe out of water. The fish knows what to do when its watery habitat disappears.

The lungfish takes a big bite of brown mud. *Squish.* The mud squeezes out through feathery gill slits under its chin. The fish wiggles forward into the hole. It takes another bite. *Squoosh.* More mud comes out through its gills. Bite by bite, the fish chews its way into the soggy ground.

Once the fish is buried, mucus oozes from its skin. The mucus dries into a leathery pod. Inside its pod, the lungfish points its nose up and continues to breathe. It slows its metabolism and digests muscle in its tail for nutrients.

The lungfish can hide this way for months, even years, under the sunbaked ground. When it hears the rains drumming on the parched earth, the fish knows it is time to come out.

FISH OUT OF WATER

Most fish can only breathe underwater. They don't have lungs. They use their gills to draw oxygen directly from the water.

A lungfish uses its gills to breathe underwater. But it can also use lungs to breathe at the surface. Thanks to its lungs, the lungfish can survive if its habitat dries up.

Seven species of lungfish live in Africa, Australia, and South America. They belong to an ancient group called the lobe-finned fishes. They look different from most fish alive today. Most fish have ray-shaped fins. Their fins are thin and flat, like a fan. But lungfish have lobe-shaped fins—fleshy and rounded.

Scientists believe that lungfish are closely related to the ancestor of all four-legged land animals. That ancestor of land animals has long since gone extinct, but its lungfish cousins are still alive.

The evolution of fish into walking animals is one of the greatest changes in the history of life. It is also a big

An African lungfish swims slowly along the bottom of a shallow pool in Mozambique.

mystery. No one knows exactly how fish did it. Could living lungfish help solve the mystery?

LOOK MA, NO FEET!

Fish changed a lot when they moved onto land 360 to 345 million years ago. They evolved larger, sturdier limbs as well as hands and feet. They developed a pelvis that was firmly attached to their spine to support their bodies on land. And they began to walk.

But which changes happened first? For a long time, scientists thought they knew. They thought fish with fins moved onto land before their bodies changed.

Then came the discovery of fossils that showed that fish were already changing, even while they still lived in water. These fossils have been found in Canada, Greenland, and Europe. (About 360 million years ago, these places were united in a single landmass that lay close to the equator.) What if fish bodies began to change underwater, before fish moved onto land?

Heather King at the University of Chicago thought maybe lungfish could help solve the mystery. Could living lungfish unravel the early steps those ancient fish took?

King wanted to investigate whether lungfish could use their fins to walk underwater. Granted, lungfish don't have sturdy limbs. They don't have feet. Their pelvis just kind of floats in their body.

But could they walk?

To find out, she used video cameras to spy on lungfish in tanks at the University of Chicago. She set up a mirror at a 45-degree angle under the lungfishes' tanks. That way, she could simultaneously film the animals from the side and underneath. This would give her a clear picture of how the fish were using their fins.

Later, watching the film, King saw lungfish using their back fins in an alternating pattern—first the left fin forward, then the right. The animals were pushing their fins along the bottom while lifting their bodies. Sometimes the fish bounded, pushing off with both back fins at the same time.

Lungfish were walking and hopping! They were using their fins just as land animals use their legs to walk and jump.

But how could the fish lift itself off the bottom on such skinny fins? King thinks the fish may have been filling their lungs with air, which made their bodies easier to lift.

King points out that her results don't *prove* fish moved onto land by walking underwater before their bodies started to change. But her discovery opens up new ideas about how the transition *might* have happened.

Maybe walking started like this: perhaps millions of years ago, ancient fish began using their fins to walk underwater. They may even have used their fins to grab onto a rock and hold themselves still so they could ambush prey that came close. It's possible that underwater, generation by generation, their bodies began to change. Only later did the animals make the move onto land.

Observing lungfish gave King new insight on an old mystery. "These animals don't have any of the things that you would think of when you think of an animal that's able to walk," she said. No attached pelvis. No sturdy limbs. No feet. But they sure can walk!

The evolution from fish to land animals is full of mystery. Scientists do not know exactly how the transition took place. This timeline shows one way the water-to-land transition might have happened.

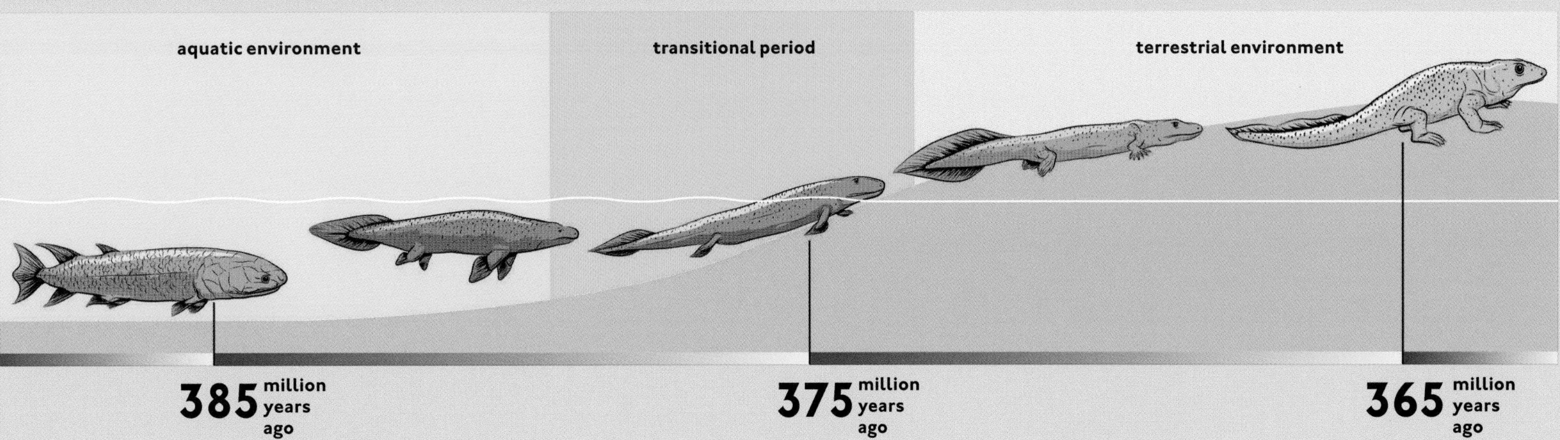

CHAPTER 5

OLD, COLD, AND SLOW

NAME: tuatara

SCIENTIFIC NAME: *Sphenodon punctatus* (SFEE-nuh-don punk-TAH-tuhs)

SIZE: up to 24 inches (61 cm)

WHERE CAN YOU FIND IT? small islands off the coast of New Zealand

HABITAT: forests and shrublands

SURVIVAL TACTIC: Tuatara have a third eye, called a parietal (puh-REYE-uh-tuhl) eye, a feature they share with most lizards. You can see the eye on top of their head, just under a layer of scaly skin. The eye cannot form an image, but it can sense sunlight and probably helps a tuatara know the time of day and the season of the year.

The sun sets on a chilly New Zealand forest, and shadows spread across the ground. A giant weta (WET-ah) cricket, the size of a sparrow, creeps down the trunk of a tree. She is ready to lay her eggs. The wingless cricket reaches the ground and wiggles her antennae. Does she sense something lurking nearby?

A spiny-backed tuatara (TOO-uh-TAHR-uh) is resting near the tree. The greenish-brown reptile turns its head and fixes one large, brown eye on the weta. When the cricket steps forward, the tuatara lunges. The reptile snatches the insect in its jaws. The cricket dies instantly. The sound of chewing carries through the forest. *Crunch, crunch, crunch.*

A tuatara looks like a chubby lizard, but it is not a lizard. Its ancestors roamed with the dinosaurs, but it is not a dinosaur. A tuatara is completely unique in the reptile world.

What makes a tuatara so strange? Take a peek into its mouth. In the bottom jaw, you'll see a single row of teeth. That looks normal. But in the top jaw, you'll see *two* rows of teeth, one behind the other.

That extra row of teeth gives tuatara a nasty bite. When a tuatara chomps down, the lower teeth fit between the upper rows. Then the jaw slides forward. A "grip and rip mechanism" is what Marc Jones calls it. Jones is an evolutionary biologist at the University College London. He says the three rows of teeth help tuatara slice through hard foods like giant crickets, seabirds, seabird eggs, beetles, and snails.

Tuatara have other weird features. They prefer the cold. That's strange for a cold-blooded reptile, which depends on heat from its surroundings to warm its body. Most reptiles can't even move if they get cold. But a tuatara can still crawl around when its body temperature drops to just 40°F (4.5°C). To cope with being chilled, a tuatara can slow its heart down to just seven beats an hour.

Tuatara live life in the slow lane. Their eggs can take fifteen months to hatch, the longest time for any reptile egg. The youngsters take thirty-five years to reach full size. Tuatara live at least one hundred years, maybe even two hundred. It's hard to know for sure because tuatara keep outliving the scientists who study them.

***Left*: Tuatara have three rows of sharp teeth for sawing through crunchy foods like this weta. *Above*: Female tuatara lay their eggs in a nest in sand. The eggs take more than a year to hatch.**

LAST OF THE BEAK-HEADS

Tuatara belong to an ancient group of reptiles known as beak-heads. About two hundred million years ago, during the time of the dinosaurs, beak-heads thrived. They swam in the ocean and crawled on land. But as early mammals began to flourish, the beak-heads dwindled and slowly disappeared—all except tuatara. They are the last of the beak-heads.

Why did tuatara survive when their relatives went extinct? Tuatara may have just gotten lucky. During the heyday of the beak-heads, New Zealand was part of the supercontinent Gondwana (which also contained Antarctica, South America, Africa, India, and Australia). But when Gondwana cracked apart, beginning 180 million years ago, New Zealand drifted away with tuatara on board. There were no mammals on the islands. No mammals to compete with tuatara for food. No mammals to dig up tuatara eggs or gobble the hatchlings. Protected by their isolation, tuatara thrived.

People often call tuatara a living fossil. But Jones does not like that phrase. It makes it sound as if tuatara hadn't changed since the dinosaur age, as if evolution had skipped over them. He knew that just because tuatara *resemble* ancient beak-heads does not mean they are *identical*. He decided to investigate how much tuatara had changed from their fossil relatives.

Jones teamed up with Carlo Meloro, a paleontologist at Liverpool John Moores University in England. The two men went looking for ancient beak-head skulls. The skulls were carefully stored at museums and personal collections in Germany, the United Kingdom, and the United States. "Some of these fossils are kind of squashed in the rock," Meloro said. But even a squashed skull can leave an accurate, side-view imprint in the rock. That accurate side-view was exactly what the scientists were looking for.

The researchers examined photographs of thirteen different species of ancient beak-head skulls. They also examined photographs of skulls of modern tuatara.

Then the scientists sat down at a computer and placed each photograph on a grid that looks like graph paper. They drew points, or dots, that corresponded to different parts of the skull. They drew one point where the jawbone ends, another point where two bones meet, and so on. In the end, they came up with a constellation of points for each skull, just as if they were making a connect-the-dots puzzle.

This constellation of points made the skulls easier to compare. Using a computer program, the scientists could measure the distances between the points. They could see how well the points from one skull lined up with the points of a different skull.

After investigating skulls this way, they discovered that tuatara looked very different from its fossil relatives. Some of the fossils had lots more teeth than modern tuatara have, and some had far fewer. The fossils had "major differences in the size and shape of the snout and position of the eye and how much space they had for jaw muscles," Jones said. Beak-heads of the past were different from modern tuatara. Evolution hadn't skipped over the tuatara at all.

The research showed that tuatara aren't a holdover from the dinosaur age. Like all animals, these living beak-heads have evolved to suit their environment. Some of the differences in their skull probably make tuatara better adapted to eat new foods—ones that ancient beak-heads didn't eat—such as giant crickets and seabird eggs, instead of small insects.

Tuatara may be well suited to their environment, but the environment is changing, and that is putting these unique reptiles at risk. The changes started about one thousand years ago, when humans first came to New Zealand. At that time, millions of tuatara roamed the islands. But people brought rats and, later, cats to the islands. These mammals dug up tuatara eggs and devoured the hatchlings. They hunted the same animals that adult tuatara ate, leaving the reptiles with less food. By the middle of the twentieth century, tuatara were extinct on New Zealand's two main islands.

Tuatara are now endangered. They live on small offshore islands, which are protected by law. People work to keep the islands free from mammal predators.

This kind of helping hand from people may be just what these old, cold reptiles need, so they can keep on crunching crickets for a long time to come.

With its duck-like bill and beaver-like tail, a platypus sure looks mixed up. But the animal is supremely adapted for its wetland habitat.

CHAPTER 6

AUSTRALIAN ODDBALL

As the sun sets over a quiet creek in eastern Australia, a furry animal creeps along the bank. About half the size of a house cat, it slinks through the tall grasses and slips silently into the water. In the light of the setting sun, it cruises along, its furred head low and flat in the water. The creature dives, and the sun glints off a ring of ripples.

After a few minutes, the flat head resurfaces, and the creature chews its catch in its leathery beak.

Yes, it's the platypus, a mixed-up critter that looks as if it were stitched together by a mad taxidermist. It has the webbed feet of an otter, the flat tail of a beaver, the bill of a duck. The platypus is so silly-looking that European scientists thought it was a hoax at first. They got their first peek at the creature in 1799, when a pickled platypus skin was shipped in a barrel to the Literary and Philosophical Society of Newcastle upon Tyne. Its arrival in England made a splash. According to one account, a female servant was carrying the barrel on her head when the bottom gave way, dousing her with strong-smelling spirits. As she stood there dripping wet, she looked down and saw the remains of "a strange creature, half bird, half beast, lying at her feet."

The platypus had arrived!

The oddball critter puzzled European scientists, who had never before seen such a hodgepodge of parts in one animal. "Most extraordinary," declared British scientist George Shaw. "The perfect resemblance of the beak of a Duck engrafted on the head of a quadruped [four-footed animal]. I almost doubt the testimony of my own eyes."

NAME: platypus

SCIENTIFIC NAME: *Ornithorhynchus anatinus* (Or-nith-o-RINK-uhs uh-NAT-i-nuhs)

SIZE: up to 40 inches (102 cm) long, including a tail up to 6 inches (15 cm) long

WHERE CAN YOU FIND IT? eastern Australia and the island of Tasmania

HABITAT: lakes, rivers, and streams

SURVIVAL TACTIC: Male platypuses have venomous spurs, about the size of a large rose thorn, on their back legs. Males use these in fights with other males during mating season. If a person gets jabbed by the spur, the venom can cause severe pain.

Although a platypus's bill looks similar to a duck's bill, the two are different. The bill of a platypus is soft and rubbery, not hard like a duck's.

Shaw poked and probed but could find no stitches or signs of fakery. Could this thing be real?

People in Australia knew the platypus was real. Indigenous Australians hunted the sleek creature with wooden spears at the water's edge. They knew it slept in a burrow by day. They knew it dove in lakes, rivers, and creeks at night, searching for worms, bugs, and crayfish to eat. Europeans, who began exploring the continent in the 1600s and later settled there, found the duckbill, or water mole, to be unusually strange—but they saw with their own eyes that it was real.

Back in Europe, as more platypuses and platypus parts arrived, scientists were forced to agree. The platypus was real. Weird but real.

But what kind of animal was it? The body was furry, and only mammals have hair or fur on their bodies. Indeed, when scientists looked at the animal's insides, they saw a skeleton that looked much like the skeletons of other mammals.

But when they inspected the platypus's back end, the mystery deepened. They found only one opening, called a cloaca (kloh-AY-kuh). The cloaca is a single hole for all body wastes, both urine and feces. The cloaca is a feature of birds and reptiles and is used for laying eggs.

Wait, *what*? Did a furry animal *lay eggs*? People in Australia claimed that it did, but some European scientists shook their heads in disbelief.

Scientists argued over how to classify the platypus. Was it a weird mammal? A furry reptile? Some entirely new kind of animal?

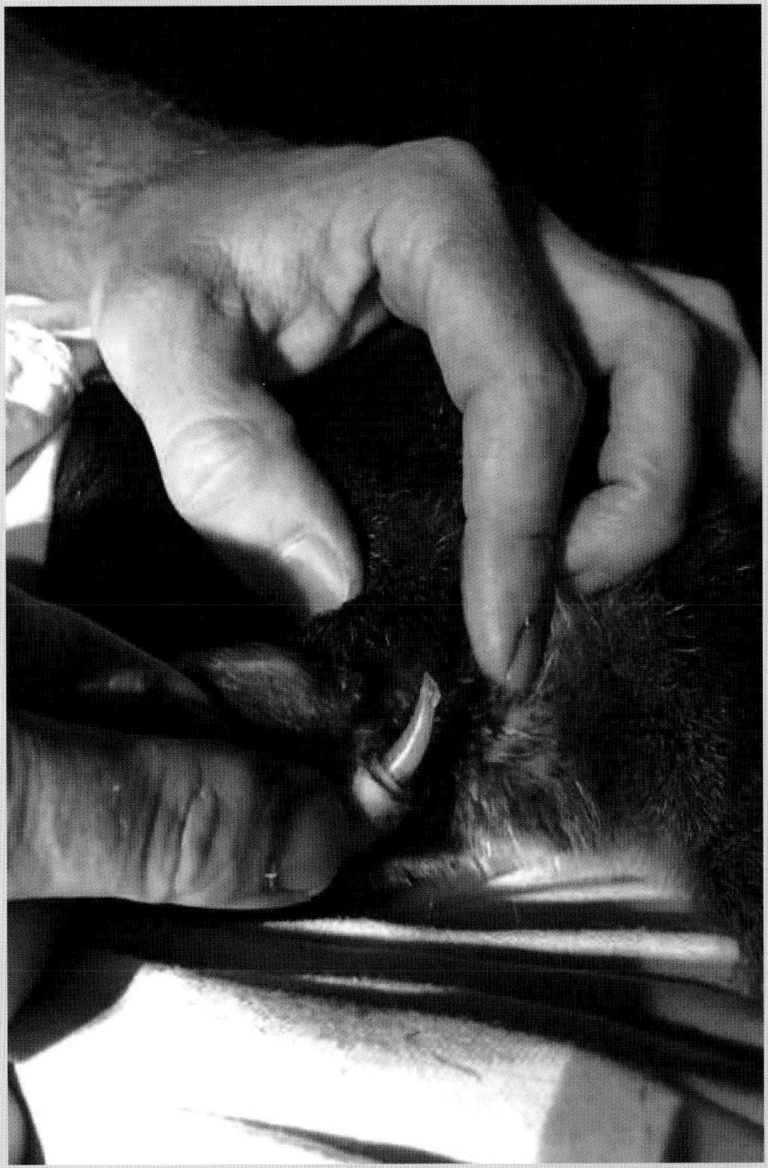

Researchers take care when handling a male platypus to avoid the venom-filled spurs on its back legs.

SOLVING THE PLATYPUS PUZZLE

It took scientists over thirty years to decide how to classify the platypus. In 1824 German scientist Johann Meckel discovered two glands just under the fur on the belly of females. They looked like the glands in mammals that produce milk. Eight years later, a Scottish soldier, Lieutenant-Colonel Lauderdale Maule, who was stationed in Australia, captured a live female and saw milk oozing from pores in her fur. That settled it. The platypus was a mammal. Only mammals feed their babies milk.

It took even longer, almost ninety years, to solve how the critter gives birth. In 1884 Scottish zoologist William Hay Caldwell set up camp on the banks of an Australian river. With the help of 150 Aboriginal people, he searched for platypus eggs. On August 24, he shot a platypus who had laid her first jelly-bean-sized egg and whose second egg was still in her body.

Caldwell had cracked the case. Platypuses lay eggs! The announcement rocked the scientific world.

Scientists place the platypus in a rare and ancient group of egg-laying mammals called monotremes (MAWN-uh-treems). The group includes four species of echidna (ih-KID-nuh), also known as spiny anteaters. Monotremes are the oldest surviving mammal group, a living link between reptiles and the rest of the mammals. They split off about 130 million years ago from early mammals. About 10 million years after that, the rest of

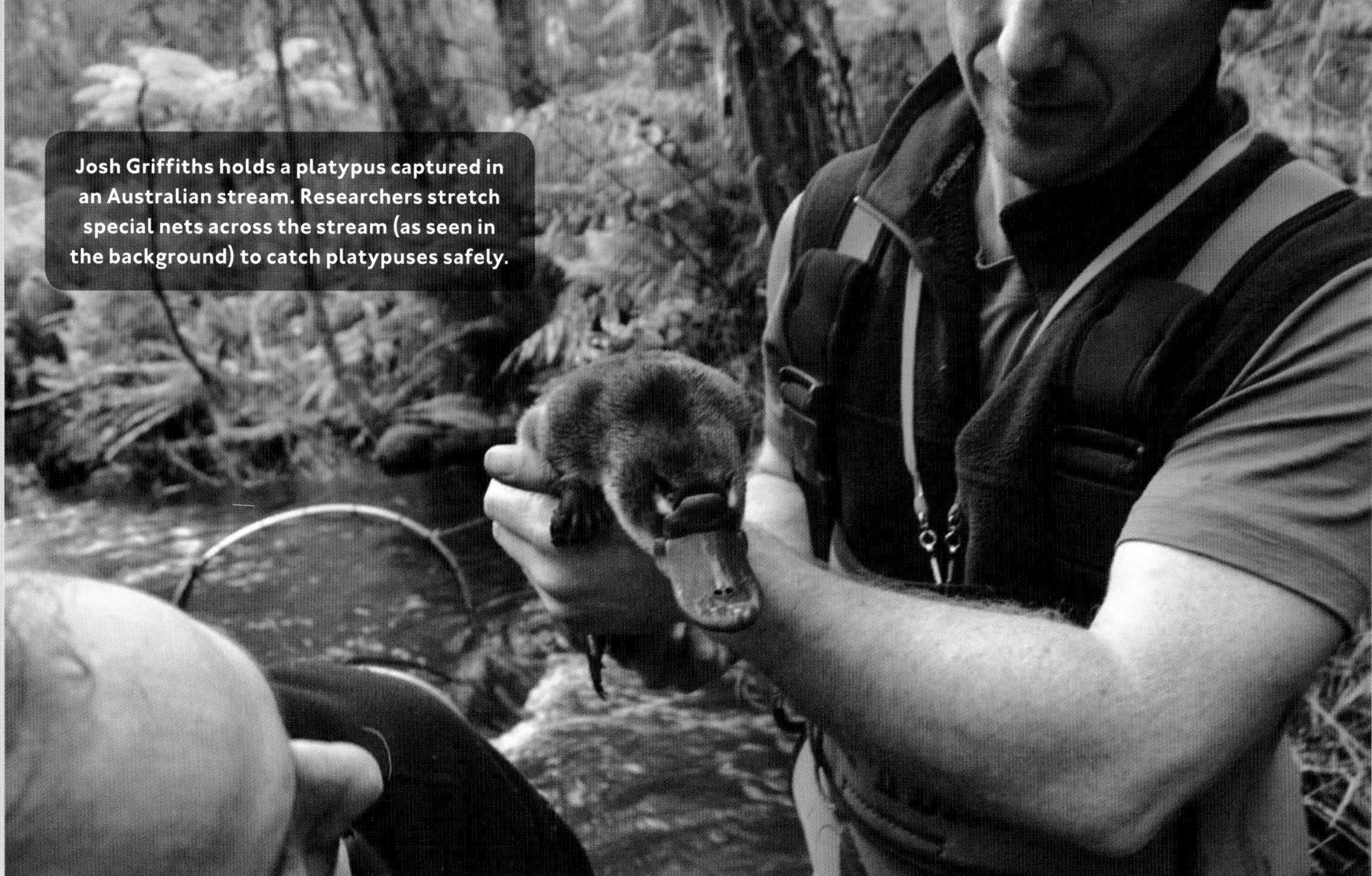
Josh Griffiths holds a platypus captured in an Australian stream. Researchers stretch special nets across the stream (as seen in the background) to catch platypuses safely.

the mammal line stopped laying eggs and began giving birth to live young.

Egg laying is only one of a platypus's weird features. The bill is another. The leathery snout is an organ for sensing electricity. When a platypus dives, it wiggles its bill back and forth in the water. The supersensitive bill can detect the tiny electric field of a shrimp flicking its tail. "The way they find their food using electroreception in their bill is completely unique to them," says Josh Griffiths.

Griffiths is a wildlife ecologist with the research organization cesar, and he has a passion for platypuses. He said that basic facts about platypuses—where they live, how long they live—remain a mystery: "Even in Australia, platypuses are just considered quite strange and weird and no one really knows much about them."

Griffiths is leading an effort to study platypuses in the wild. He and his team set up nets in Australian streams. If a platypus swims into the net, it gets funneled into a chamber. The researchers inspect the nets at night to see what they've caught.

Each captured platypus gets a health check and a microchip implanted under its skin. The microchip has a

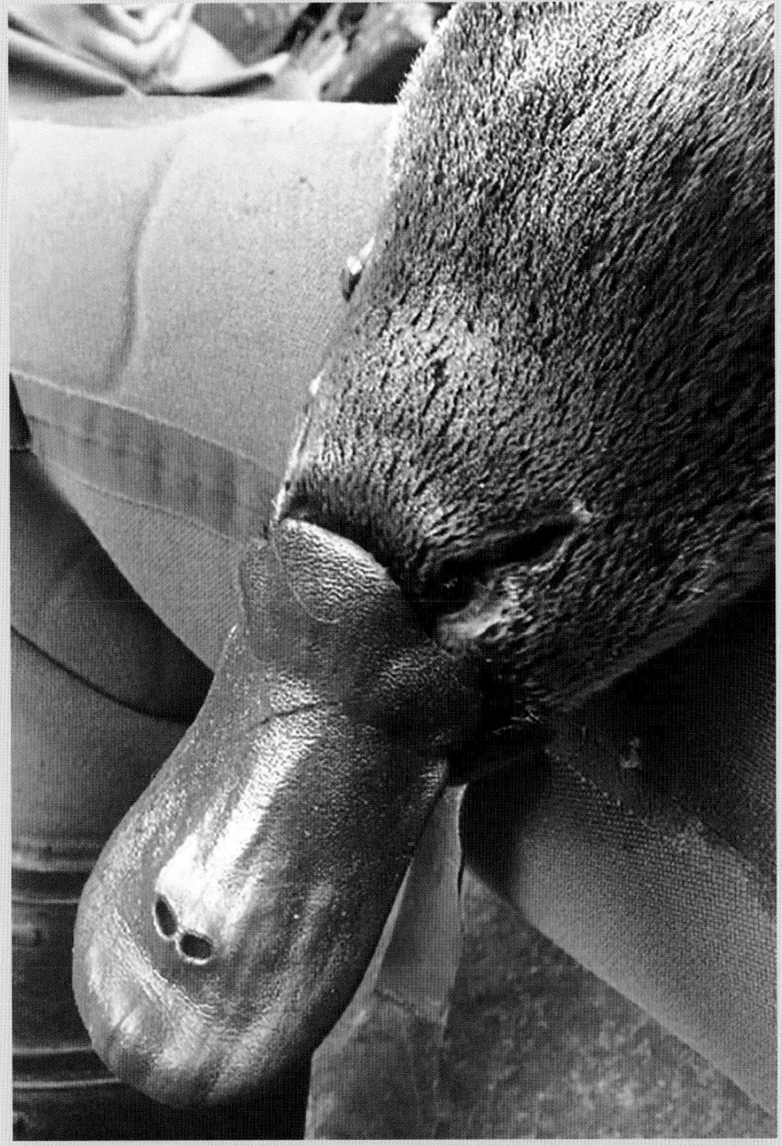

Each platypus gets a health check and a microchip before its release. The microchip allows researchers to know if they've caught that platypus before.

bar code that identifies the platypus. It allows the team to know if they've caught the same platypus before—and has led to some unexpected discoveries.

"A couple of years ago we caught the oldest known male platypus," Griffiths said. Most platypuses are expected to live no more than twelve years. But this guy had been alive for so long that he was caught twice. The first time he was caught and microchipped as a youngster, just eighteen months old. When he was caught for the second time years later, he had reached the grand old age of twenty-one. That made him the oldest male platypus on record.

Griffiths said their research is showing that platypuses are disappearing from places they used to live. The mammals are no longer hunted, but humans can harm them in other ways, like polluting their habitat. He explained, "These animals are very good at getting things like rubber bands and hair ties and plastic rings caught over their heads."

He hopes the research will alert people to the need to protect the Australian oddball and its habitat. "They're one of the most unique creatures on the planet," he said. "That in itself is worth saving."

CHAPTER 7

A BITE LIKE A SNAKE

With gnarly toes, a long bendable nose, and an odor like a goat, a solenodon is one unique mammal!

In the dark of night, a prehistoric mammal waddles through the forest. Its tail is long. Its eyes are beady. Its toes are gnarly. As its sniffs the ground, its long nose bends from side to side.

This is a solenodon (soh-LEN-uh-dahn), and it's one of the weirdest mammals alive.

The rabbit-sized animal sniffs through fallen leaves. It stops and digs with its long claws. It pokes its long nose into the soft ground, searching for something tasty. It unearths a wiggly earthworm. The worm thrashes and flops in the earth. The solenodon bites into the worm and injects venom. The worm stops wiggling, and the solenodon eats.

The Hispaniolan solenodon lives only on the Caribbean island of Hispaniola. A second species, the Cuban solenodon, lives on the nearby island of Cuba. The creatures split off from the rest of the mammal line seventy-six million years ago when dinosaurs still ruled Earth.

What makes this mammal so wonderfully weird? Let's start with the nipples. Like all mammals, solenodons feed their young milk. But they do it as no other mammal does. The female's nipples are located so far down her belly that they are almost on her backside. That's right, her nipples are near her butt.

Then there is the snout. The solenodon is the only animal with a bone in its nose. The bone fits into a ball-and-socket joint, just like your shoulder does. That's why a solenodon can wiggle its snout from side to side as it searches for food.

NAME: Hispaniolan solenodon

SCIENTIFIC NAME: *Solenodon paradoxus* (soh-LEN-uh-dahn payr-uh-DOK-suhs)

SIZE: up to 28 inches (71 cm) including up to 10 inches (25 cm) of tail

HABITAT: forests and shrublands

WHERE CAN YOU FIND IT? the Caribbean island of Hispaniola

SURVIVAL TACTIC: Solenodons spend their days in underground burrows and only come out at night. This explains why people rarely see them. It also may explain how they survived the meteorite that struck Earth sixty-five million years ago. Maybe solenodons stayed alive by hiding out under the ground.

Finally, let's talk venom. A solenodon delivers its venom just as a snake does—using its grooved teeth to inject venom into its prey. (The word *solenodon* means "grooved teeth.") Unlike snakes, solenodons inject venom from their bottom teeth rather than their upper teeth. Don't worry, a solenodon only attacks when defending itself and rarely goes after people. Scientists don't actually know why the animal makes venom. They suspect the venom is intended for its prey, which includes worms, insects, snails, small reptiles, and frogs.

Millions of years ago, venomous mammals may have been common. Scientists think most mammals lost their venom because they had other ways of catching and killing prey. But maybe they started out like the solenodon—a mammal that bites like a snake.

HUNTING GHOSTS

The island of Hispaniola was once full of unique mammals—ground sloths, a monkey, two species of solenodons. Then humans came to the islands six thousand years ago, arriving from South America. Europeans followed fifteen hundred years later. People chopped down forests, destroying the animal's habitats. They brought cats, dogs, and mongooses—predators that hunted and killed native mammals. Most of the island's mammals quickly went extinct. But somehow, solenodons survived.

In 1907 explorer and naturalist Alpheus Hyatt Verrill went to the island to track down a solenodon. Fellow scientists called his quest hopeless. One told him he was "as likely to secure specimens of a ghost."

Verrill managed to catch a single solenodon. Over the years, sightings remained rare. By the 1970s, solenodons were thought to be extinct on the island. Then a few animals were spotted in 1974 and 1975.

The ghosts were alive!

The species was believed to be teetering on the brink of extinction. Then came 2009. That's when scientists from the United Kingdom and Dominican Republic teamed up to study the rare mammal. Jose Nuñez-Miño, an ecologist, was a field manager for the project.

"We were told it was going to be a very hard mammal to study and we'd be lucky if we saw it a handful of times," Nuñez-Miño said. "Once we started looking, it was far more common than we imagined."

Locating the secretive creatures took some detective work. Solenodons are nocturnal, so people rarely see them. Local guides taught the researchers how to identify signs of the animals.

Clue number one: nose pokes. These small, cone-shaped holes are made when a solenodon digs and pokes its long nose into the ground.

Clue number two: a stinky smell. Solenodons spend the daytime in underground dens. An active burrow smells something like a goat or maybe a wet dog.

When researchers found these signs, they knew they were on the trail. Next, they set up infrared camera traps

Left: In the Dominican Republic, a researcher examines a solenodon. *Above*: To find a solenodon in the forest, researchers look for nose pokes. These small holes are made when the animal sticks its long nose in the ground.

in the area. The cameras filmed any animals that crossed in front of the cameras at night. The team saw plenty of solenodons sniffing around in the darkness.

The last step was to catch live animals. But how do you catch a solenodon? That took some trial and error.

They tried luring the animals with food. But solenodons "just refused to go to the food," Nuñez-Miño said. "I mean that just never worked."

Next, they tried traps. "That again didn't work. They didn't go for those at all."

The team eventually learned to sit in the darkness and wait to hear the quiet rustle of a solenodon moving through the brush.

Then the chase would begin. A team member would plunge into thick undergrowth, bare hands grabbing in the darkness. Sometimes the person came out empty-handed. Other times, they held a blinking solenodon by its tail.

The team then weighed and measured the animals. They outfitted some solenodons with a radio-tagged collar before freeing them. That allowed the team to track each animal's movements in the wild.

The project revealed that solenodons are actually pretty common. The team found them living in all sorts of habitats: dry lowlands, pine forests, and high up in the mountains. Nuñez-Miño said, "It's a really positive conservation story."

It's also an opportunity. People have a chance to protect these unique mammals and their habitat, and ensure this survivor keeps going far into the future.

CONCLUSION

NATURE'S SURVIVORS

Human beings are changing land, water, and air all over the planet. Even places that seem untouched, like this rain forest reserve in Brazil, are feeling the effects.

Living fossils are survivors. Solenodons and tuatara withstood the meteorite that wiped out the dinosaurs. Horseshoe crabs and nautiluses have survived all five mass extinctions—they have prowled the planet for nearly half a billion years.

Human beings are relative newcomers. Modern humans appeared on the planet just two hundred thousand years ago. But the story of living fossils is now our story. Even though we have lived on Earth a much shorter time than they have, we share this world with them, and we determine their future.

Our planet is entering what some biologists call the sixth extinction. This new mass extinction is one of our own making. Humans are changing the land, the oceans, and the atmosphere at an unprecedented rate. Many animals are not able to evolve quickly enough to adapt and are at risk of extinction.

Living fossils are among the ones most in danger. "We have an impact on these animals," said Basil. "The nautilus lineage survived five hundred million years, and in forty years, we've almost decimated [destroyed] them. They've survived five mass extinctions, and they're not surviving us."

If people don't act to protect living fossils, we could lose creatures that have lived on the planet for tens or hundreds of millions of years. Without our help, ancient lineages could vanish from the world forever.

These lineages may be old, but scientists have only studied them for a short time. We have much to learn about these animals. They have much to teach us about life—how it was in the past, how it is now, and how it will be in the future. Our job is to keep them alive and thriving.

AUTHOR'S NOTE

I've long been fascinated by living things that challenge our ideas about how life works. So of course I was drawn to living fossils. They're the ultimate rule breakers!

I began by sketching out a list of possible animals to include in this book. I read scientific articles on the subject. But I quickly hit a roadblock; I found out that scientists disagreed among themselves over what makes something a living fossil and which animals qualified.

I felt I needed a clear definition to help me choose which creatures to include in the book. After researching and thinking about it, I decided it wasn't enough that an animal closely resembled its fossil relatives. The species needed to be the last, or nearly the last, of its kind. It had to possess traits that are now uncommon in the animal kingdom.

With this definition in hand, I began to whittle down my list of animals. From my initial list, only two species—horseshoe crabs and tuatara—made the final cut. But I discovered wonderful new animals to include, including one I hadn't previously heard of. I'm looking at you, solenodon!

I didn't set out to write a book about conservation, but once I began talking to the dedicated men and women who study these animals, I realized that most of these species are endangered by human activity. And so conservation became a core part of the story.

The best part of this project was getting to talk with scientists from around the world. Thanks to the internet, I was able to speak with experts on four continents. I am extremely grateful to these passionate people for taking time to talk with me, share their knowledge and insights into these animals, and to review parts of the book. I send my sincere thanks to Jennifer Basil, Jeak Ling Ding, Josh Griffiths, Marc Jones, Heather King, Carlos Meloro, and Jose Nuñez-Miño. Thank you for all you are doing to study and protect these wonderfully weird and important creatures!

SOURCE NOTES

17 Jeak Ling Ding, personal communication with the author, June 3, 2019.

17 Ding.

17 Ding.

20 Jennifer A. Basil, personal communication with the author, May 17, 2019.

21 Basil.

21 Basil.

21 Basil.

25 Heather King, personal communication with the author, May 16, 2019.

27 Marc Jones, personal communication with the author, May 2, 2019.

28–29 Carlo Meloro, personal communication with the author, May 9, 2019.

29 Jones, personal communication.

31 Ann Moyal, "This Highly Interesting Novelty," in *Platypus: The Extraordinary Story of How a Curious Creature Baffled the World* (Washington, DC: Smithsonian Institution, 2001), 5

31–32 Harry Burrell, "Discovery and Early Descriptions," in *The Platypus: Its Discovery, Zoological Position, Form and Characteristics, Habits, Life History, Etc.* (Sydney: Angus & Robertson, 1927), 19.

34 Josh Griffiths, personal communication with the author, May 9, 2019.

34 Griffiths.

35 Griffiths.

35 Griffiths.

35 Griffiths.

36 Grace Constantino and Alexis Mychajliw, "A Window into the Past, Present, and Future of Caribbean Mammals," *Biodiversity Heritage Library* (blog), accessed June 28, 2019, https://blog.biodiversitylibrary.org/2019/06/bhl-and-caribbean-mammals.html.

38 Jose Nuñez-Miño, personal communication with the author, June 25, 2019.

39 Nuñez-Miño.

39 Nuñez-Miño.

39 Nuñez-Miño.

41 Basil, personal communication.

GLOSSARY

amphibian: a cold-blooded vertebrate animal that spends part of its life cycle in water. Frogs and salamanders are amphibians.

arthropod: a large group of invertebrate animals with a segmented body, jointed limbs, and a hard outer shell. Insects, spiders, lobsters, and crabs are arthropods.

bacteria: extremely small single-celled living things. Although many bacteria are useful, some can cause disease.

cephalopod: a group of mollusks that has muscular tentacles. Squids, octopuses, cuttlefishes, and nautiluses are cephalopods.

climate: the average weather in a particular place over a long time

evolution: a scientific idea that different living things are descended from other kinds of living things from earlier times. The differences are due to inherited changes that accumulate over many generations.

extinct: no longer existing. An animal species becomes extinct when it has no living members.

feces: solid animal waste; also known as excrement or poop

gill: an organ used by water-dwelling animals, such as fish, to obtain oxygen from the water for breathing

gland: a structure in the body that makes and releases a substance

habitat: the type of place where an animal naturally lives

invertebrate: an animal that lacks a backbone. Worms, clams, insects, and octopuses are invertebrates.

lineage: a line of descent, connecting a living thing back to an ancestor

mammal: a warm-blooded vertebrate that has hair or fur and nourishes its young with milk. Cats, dogs, and human beings are mammals.

meteorite: a rocky object from space that reaches Earth's surface

mollusk: a large group of related invertebrate animals with soft bodies and often having an external shell. Snails, clams, and octopuses are mollusks.

mucus: a sticky, slippery substance made by animals

natural selection: a natural process in which organisms best adapted to their environment survive and produce young, while poorly adapted organisms die

nocturnal: active at night

photosynthesis: the process by which green plants make carbohydrates from water and carbon dioxide in the air, in the presence of sunlight

phytoplankton: floating tiny plant life in a body of water

predator: an animal that captures and eats other animals

prey: an animal that is captured and eaten by predators

reptile: a cold-blooded vertebrate with scales on its body. Lizards, snakes, turtles, crocodiles, and tuatara are reptiles.

sedimentary: formed from sand, mud, or stones that are laid down in layers by water or wind

segmented: divided into or made of segments

spawn: to deposit or fertilize eggs

species: a specific kind of living thing

synthetic: produced artificially, not by natural processes

trait: a characteristic of an animal that can be inherited from its parents

venom: poison produced by an animal and passed to a victim by biting or stinging

vertebrate: an animal with a backbone and a skeleton made of bone

MORE TO EXPLORE

Books

Johnson, Rebecca L. *When Lunch Fights Back: Wickedly Clever Animal Defenses*. Minneapolis: Millbrook, 2015.

Ridley, Kimberley. *Extreme Survivors: Animals That Time Forgot*. Thomaston, ME: Tilbury House, 2017.

Walker, Sally M. *Fossil Fish Found Alive: Discovering the Coelacanth*. Minneapolis: Carolrhoda Books, 2002.

Videos

"Horseshoe Crabs Saved My Life"
https://www.youtube.com/watch?v=90LTtKIFY8U
Learn more about horseshoe crabs and how their blue blood saves lives.

Lungfish Walking
https://www.pnas.org/content/108/52/21146/tab-figures-data
Scroll down on the page to see four short videos taken by Heather King that show lungfish walking and bounding.

"The Nautilus Will Make You Rethink Intelligence"
https://www.youtube.com/watch?v=5UYFCiV0r4c
In this short interview with Jennifer Basil, you can see nautiluses swimming in tanks in her lab.

"A Night with the Platypus Guy"
https://www.youtube.com/watch?v=A7TmQIIVwWc
Spend a night with Josh Griffiths as he catches platypuses in Australian streams.

"The Slimy, Deadly Velvet Worm"
https://www.youtube.com/watch?v=LY8TgD6-7kg
Watch the velvet worm's gooey way of capturing prey.

"Solenodon Hunt: Face to Face with a Bizarre Beast"
http://wildlife.durrell.org/latest/news-bites/solenodon-an-extraordinary-mammal-comes-into-the-spotlight/
Come along as researchers head into the Hispaniolan forest at night and come face-to-face with a solenodon.

"Tuatara All the Way Down"
https://www.pbs.org/video/tuatara-all-the-way-down-8xkhqn/
Find out more about the tuatara, sole survivor of a 220-million-year-old branch of reptiles.

"West African Lungfish"
https://www.nationalgeographic.org/media/west-african-lungfish/
Watch lungfish burrow into the mud when their marsh dries up and rise from the ground when the rains return.

Websites

Animals Past and Present
http://extension.illinois.edu/animals/intro.cfm
Get better acquainted with the long history of animal life on Earth.

The Horseshoe Crab
http://horseshoecrab.org/
A comprehensive website about horseshoe crabs, with lots of ways for you to learn more and get involved.

Platypus
https://www.nationalgeographic.com/animals/mammals/p/platypus/
Learn more about the mixed-up mammal that scientists first thought was a hoax.

Save the Nautilus
http://www.savethenautilus.com/
Get to know the nautilus on this website started by two eleven-year-olds, Josiah Utsch and Ridgely Kelly. You can learn about the shelled sea creature and how you can help save it.

SELECTED BIBLIOGRAPHY

Crook, Robyn J., and Jennifer A. Basil. "Flexible Spatial Orientation and Navigational Strategies in Chambered Nautilus." *Ethology* 119 (2012): 77–85.

Fortey, Richard. *Horseshoe Crabs and Velvet Worms: The Story of the Animals and Plants That Time Has Left Behind.* New York: Random House, 2012.

Jones, Marc E. H., Paul O'Higgins, Michael J. Fagan, Susan E. Evans, and Neil Curtis. "Shearing Mechanics and the Influence of a Flexible Symphysis During Oral Food Processing in Sphenodon (Lepidosauria: Rhynchocephalia)." *Anatomical Record* 295, no. 7 (2012): 1075–1091.

King, Heather M., Neil H. Shubin, Michael I. Coates, and Melina E. Hale. "Behavioral Evidence for the Evolution of Walking and Bounding before Terrestriality in Sarcopterygian Fishes." *Proceedings of the National Academy of Sciences* 108, no. 52 (2011): 21146–21151.

Li, Peng, Bow Ho, and Jeak Ling Ding. "Biotechnology Efforts to Conserve Horseshoe Crabs through the Development of Recombinant Factor C-Based Endotoxin Test." In Ruth H. Carmichael, Mark L. Botton, Paul K. S. Shin, and Siu Gin Cheung. *Changing Global Perspectives on Horseshoe Crab Biology, Conservation and Management.* Cham, Switzerland: Springer, 2015, 501–512.

Meloro, Carlo, and Marc E. H. Jones. "Tooth and Cranial Disparity in the Fossil Relatives of Sphenodon (Rhynchocephalia) Dispute the Persistent 'Living Fossil' Label." *Journal of Evolutionary Biology* 25 (2012): 2194–2209.

Moyal, Ann. *Platypus: The Extraordinary Story of How a Curious Creature Baffled the World.* Washington, DC: Smithsonian Institution, 2001.

Turvey, Sam T., Rosalind J. Kennerley, Jose M. Nuñez-Miño, and Richard P. Young. "The Last Survivors: Current Status and Conservation of the Non-Volant Land Mammals of the Insular Caribbean." *Journal of Mammalogy* 98, no. 4 (2017): 918–936.

Ward, Peter. *On Methuselah's Trail: Living Fossils and the Great Extinctions.* New York: W. H. Freeman, 1992.

INDEX

PHOTO ACKNOWLEDGMENTS

Image credits: johan10/iStock/Getty Images, p. 1; Photo courtesy Greg J. Barord/Center for Biological Diversity, pp. 2, 18, 20, 48; Bazzano Photography/Alamy Stock Photo, p. 4; Science Photo Library/ STEVE GSCHMEISSNER/Brand X Pictures/Getty Images, p. 6; wannasak saetia/Shutterstock.com, p. 8; Photo credit John Dreyer/Getty Images, p. 12; jtstewartphoto/Stockphoto/Getty Images, p. 14 (top); ImageBROKER/Alamy Stock Photo, p. 14 (bottom); Timothy Fadek/Corbis/Getty Images, p. 16 (right); © Piotr Naskrecki/Minden Pictures, p. 22; Tom McHugh/Science Source, p. 24; Laura Westlund/ Independent Picture Service, p. 25; Molly Marshall/Alamy Stock Photo, p. 26; © Mark Moffett/Minden Pictures, p. 28 (left); Bob Gibbons/Alamy Stock Photo, p. 28 (right); Greg Wyncoll/Shutterstock.com, p. 30; © D. Parer and E. Parer-Cook/Minden Pictures, p. 32; Josh Griffiths, pp. 33, 34, 35; © Gregory Guida/Minden Pictures, pp. 36, 39 (left); Courtesy of Joe Nuñez-Miño/Durrell Wildlife Conservation Trust, p. 39 (right); Vitor Marigo/Getty Images, p. 40; David Santiago Garcia/Aurora Photos/Getty Images, p. 42; Alizada Studios/Shutterstock.com, p. 47. Cover: SCIEPRO/SCIENCE PHOTO LIBRARY/Getty Images; Gustavo Zoppello Toffoli/Shutterstock.com.